Choose a topic and start to practise writing. Each booklet has a theme to help you start to write…stories, reports, articles, letters and many more. Start collecting them now.

Guinea Pig creative writing booklets also provide extra practice for children who have completed:

- Creative Story Writing ISBN: 9780955831508
- Persuasive Writing & Argument ISBN: 9780955831515
- Information Writing ISBN: 9780955831522

They are for:

* children who are working at Key Stage 2 of the National Curriculum, levels 3-5 (in Years 5 and 6 of primary school),
* children who are working at Key Stage 3, levels 3-5 (Years 7 and 8 of Secondary School).

They provide practice for all 9-13 year olds, especially children taking 11+ examinations.

Written by Sally A. Jones and Amanda C. Jones

Published by GUINEA PIG EDUCATION

2 Cobs Way,
New Haw,
Addlestone,
Surrey,
KT15 3AF.

www.guineapigeducation.co.uk

Let's **learn** to *write* <u>non-fiction</u>.

When you *write non-fiction*, <u>**you may write**</u>:

- a police report

- an accident leaflet

- a newspaper report

- an information leaflet

- instructions

- a diary entry

<u>You must decide</u>:

1. Who will be my target audience?

2. Who will read this writing?

3. What is the purpose of my writing?

If you are writing a police statement, your writing will be <u>**formal**</u>, or impersonal. It will be the language of a newsreader.

Remember, informal or personal language is chatty and friendly and may include slang words.

Plan your non-fiction writing:

<table>
<tr><td>

PARAGRAPH 1

- Write an introduction to set the scene.

</td><td>

- Who are the people involved?

- When did it happen?

- Where did it happen?

- Why did it happen?

- What time did the event take place?

</td></tr>
<tr><td>

PARAGRAPH 2, 3, 4...

- To **INFORM**: Tell the main events in the order they happened in several paragraphs. Pick out the most important details, so the events unfold for the reader.

- To **EXPLAIN**: Say how and why you think something happened and how it affected other people. What caused the accident and the effects it had on others.

</td><td>

- Use new paragraphs for change of place, time and subject.

- Use connectives or conjunctions:

  - *and or but (to join compound sentences)*
  - *or, so, if, when, while, after, before, because, unless, until, whereas, although (to join complex sentences)*
  - *use pronouns - who, which, whose, what, that*
  - *to link ideas use - firstly, later, therefore, on the other hand, at that moment, by this time, next, soon...*

- Use a range of sentences – simple, compound and complex sentences

</td></tr>
<tr><td>

Conclusion

- In conclusion, the writer makes a comment - '*in my opinion*...'. Draw the facts to a conclusion with a comment.

</td><td>

</td></tr>
</table>

Imagine

You were driving to your karate class. You saw the horses running down the road. A white van swerved to avoid the animals, but it crashed into a tree. Fortunately, the driver was not badly hurt and neither were the horses. You were the first person to see the accident, so you have been asked to write a detailed account of what you saw. Write a report for the police.

Rushford Police Department

POLICE REPORT

Case No: 3365548

Date: 2nd April 2015

Reporting Officer: John Smith

Witness: Catrina Colins

Incident: Car accident

Time of Accident: 6pm

My mum was driving me to my karate lesson, taking the normal route. As we went round a bend in the road, we saw two horses galloping towards us. The red car, in front of us, was going quite fast. He swerved violently to avoid hitting the horses, but lost control of the car and hit a tree.

We stopped our car immediately by the side of the road and went over to the elderly driver, who had short grey hair. The front of the car was badly dented, the headlamps were smashed and the windscreen was shattered. There were fragments of glass everywhere. I thought the driver was badly injured, but he said that he was fine. Then, he struggled to get out of the vehicle, which was crushed like a tin can and stood shaking his head by the side of the road. His grey suit was also covered in glass. Mum rang 999 to call the police.

By this time, the horses, terrified by the experience, had galloped further down the road at a fast pace. The traffic had come to a halt and there was a long queue. A lady, who was used to horses, attempted to catch them and she managed to get them on to the side of the road. At that moment, there was the sound of emergency vehicles approaching. After this, a police car, an ambulance and a local farmer with a horse box arrived one after the other. A policeman directed the traffic and waved us on, but I was quite late for my karate class.

A deer runs across the road and causes an accident. Write a police report.

Rushford Police Department
POLICE REPORT

Case No: ....   **Date:** ....

Reporting Officer: John Smith   **Witness:** *(Your name)* ....

Incident: ....   **Time of Accident:** ....

....

....

....

....

....

....

....

....

....

....

....

....

....

....

....

....

....

....

Use these sentences to help you write some more accident reports.

Imagine you see an incident.

- Where were you going?
- Why?
- Who were you with?
- When was it? What time of the day was it?

- What did you see?
- What happened next...?
- ...and what were the consequences?
- Was there anyone else involved?

- What was the driver like? *(age and appearance)*
- How damaged was the car?
- Was there: glass on the road?
    - dents in the door?
    - serious damage (smashed up like a tin can)?
- Give details.

- What did you do next?
- Was the driver unhurt and able to get out?
- Was he injured?
- Did you call an ambulance?
- What did the other witnesses do?
- Which other emergency services attended?

- What happened in the end?
- What was the outcome?
- What in your opinion caused the accident?

Have you witnessed or been involved in an accident?
Write an accident report.

Write police statements for some more <u>incidents</u> you have seen.

Here are some topic sentences of some crime reports. Complete them. A topic sentence is the first sentence of a paragraph and tells you what it will be about.

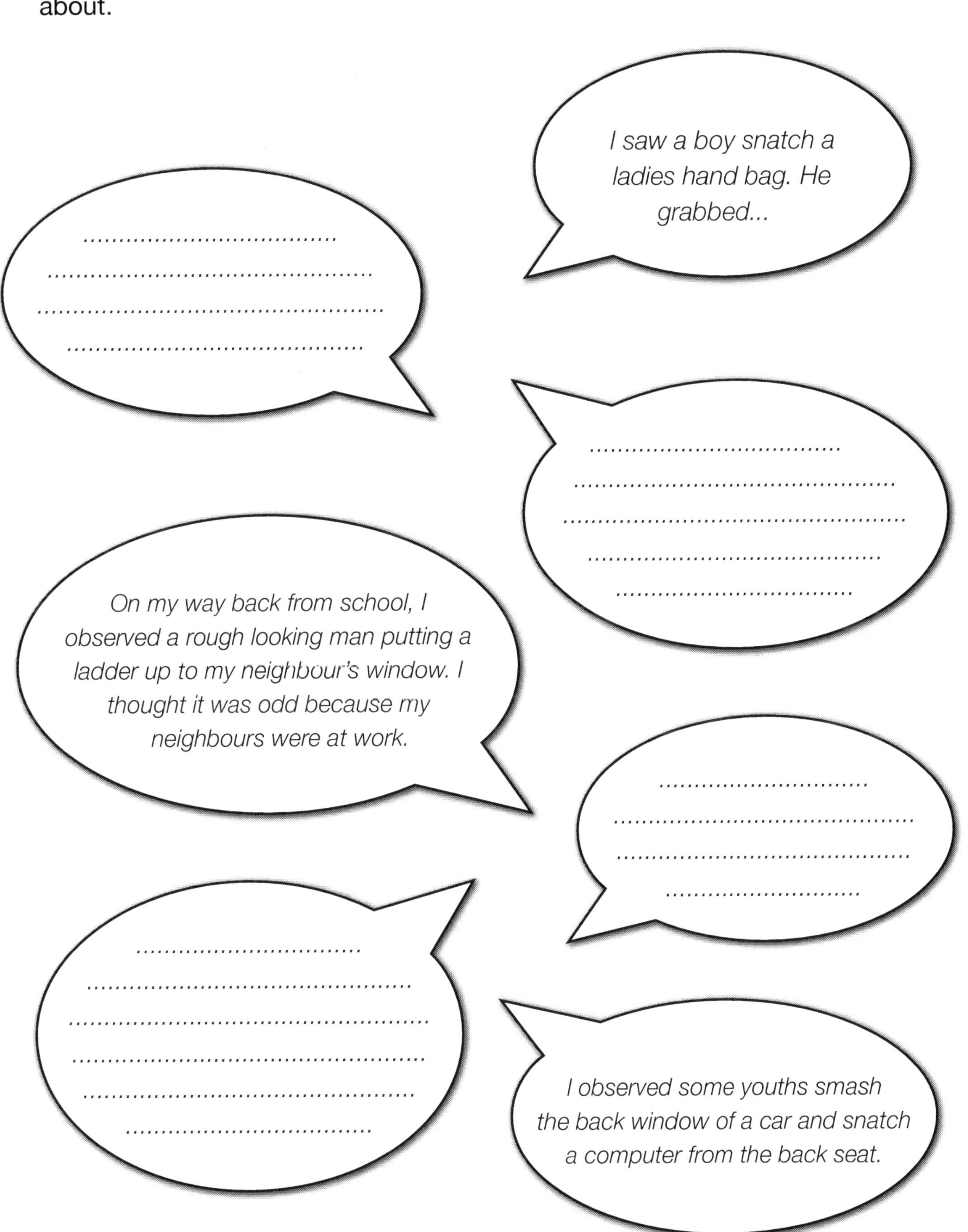

Read these crime scenarios

You awake in the middle of the night. It is 3 am. There are some youths on the garage roof next door. They are signalling to a boy on the ground. Why are they there at this time? You ring...

The police arrive in a few minutes – their sirens are silent, but their lights are flashing. Is there a chase? They apprehend some suspicious characters and ask them questions. What is the outcome? Have they stolen something? Are they told to go home or hand cuffed and put into the police car?

A milk thief is stealing milk from doorsteps and sometimes he or she throws the empty bottle on the lawn. Early one morning, the thief follows the milk delivery van and steals milk from the cart. The milkman sees the thief and rings...

You look out of your window and see a man scaling a high wall at the back of your garden. Another man is flashing a torch on the ground. Are the police conducting a search? You see the criminal is escaping. You ring...

You pull back the curtain, but there is a man on the flat roof. Your eyes meet for one moment and then he scarpers, sliding down the drainpipe. Your ring...

You go to feed your rabbit and guinea pig, but they have disappeared. Ring...

You are a builder, who is working in a house quite late in the evening. The owners are away. Some bad kids enter the property to get their ball, but they refuse to leave. You shout at them to go, but they start to get nasty and throw eggs at the house. You ring...

An old lady has been taken to hospital suddenly, but she left money lying round her house. Thieves break in. Neighbours report strange noises in the empty house. They ring...

A secretary leaves her office for a minute to use the photo copying machine. A window cleaner sees her bag and takes the opportunity to steal fifty pounds. Later, she is in the shops and searches her bag for the cash – her money is missing. She rings the police... The police interview her. What questions do they ask? What information does she give them? Can she describe the man?

You return to your holiday apartment in France, to find your jewellery, a watch and some perfume missing. The door is ajar and the curtains crumpled. Has there been a robbery? You try to explain the situation to the French police, but they don't speak much English.

Now develop the stories on the last few pages into police reports. Have you seen any other crimes that you can write reports on?

Write your police report here.

A _break_ in _(a recount)_

I remember the brisk walk back to the car, that evening, after we came out of the cinema. It was a cold and frosty night with a biting cold wind so I cuddled up to my dad to keep warm. "My friends will be dead jealous," I whispered in his ear, "when they hear I've been to see the new film, 'The Zombie Ghost', with Chad Brit in it. He's a really famous celebrity. What was your favourite part?" I asked as we arrived back at the car.

 Dad unlocked the door and we clambered in. It was as icy as a freezer and the windows had frosted up. Dad was searching for the de-icer scraper when suddenly, someone banged on the side window. It certainly startled us.
"Do you realise the back window is broken?" shouted a young man, "it's been smashed." Dad shot out of the car at great speed and raced round to the back. I followed. The window was shattered; fragments of glass were everywhere.
"Oh no," he gasped. "My computer has been stolen and all my work correspondence have gone! What am I going to do?"

It was at least an hour before the policeman came. "It's the usual story," he exclaimed, "every night a car gets broken into in this street, while someone is at the cinema or the theatre. It will be those lads on bikes. They are a cunning couple of crooks. They are well known in this area but as yet, we do not have enough evidence to arrest them." He examined the crime scene. "You see the council refuse to put CCTV cameras up," he added. Then, he instructed me to jump into the police car and we drove fast to the police station. Dad drove slowly behind in our smashed up car. It took hours to make a statement and to write a detailed list of everything that had been stolen.

After an hour, we were free to make our journey home. It was awful; the film was a distant memory. An icy chill blasted through the broken window and we sat pale and expressionless like two zombie ghosts. I had a sad, sinking sort of feeling. Why did the evening have to end like this? Then, the catchy ring tone of Dad's mobile began to play.
"You won't know me…," uttered the voice on the other end of the phone, "…but I've just found a pile of your work papers under my car, with your phone number on them. I thought it was rubbish, but then I realised that it belonged to someone."
"Where are you?" said Dad. "I'll come immediately."

Write a recount or a story of a crime incident that has happened to you.

1st PERSON	3rd PERSON

1st PERSON

- Introduce character, setting and plot

1) You have been on a day trip to London. You are excited about the day out.

  - Where do you go?
  - Why?
  - Who are you with?
  - What do you see?
  - How do you feel?

What happens next?

You come back to your car. The window is smashed. Your dad's computer has been stolen:

  - How do you feel now?
  - What do you do?

2) Build up tension. You wait for the police.

What does the policeman say when he arrives?
You go to the police station with him and he completes a crime report:

  - What has been stolen?
  - What damage has been done?

3) How does the story wind up? A member of the public rings you up to say they've found your stolen items:

  - What do they say?
  - What do you do?

3rd PERSON

- Introduce character, setting and plot

1) A car is parked on the cliff top while the owners go to a firework display in the lower gardens.

  While the family enjoy themselves, a vandal smashes the car window with a sharp object. He steals a designer bag, C.Ds, a leather jacket and some bags of shopping.

What happens next?

  A passer by hears the breaking glass. He yells, "What do you think you're doing?" He chases the robber who throws the loot over the fence and dashes up an alleyway of some flats.

2) Build up tension.

  When the owners return, they see the smashed window. They see a police car with flashing lights. There has been a break in – it's their car! What has been stolen. Panic!

3) How does the story wind up?

  The family go to the police station to make a statement. The phone rings. A squad car has been patrolling the area. They have found a bag, by some flats, behind the hedge. The contents match the description of the missing items. How do they feel?

Now write the story you planned.

THE DAILY NEWS

ALL ABOUT THE BIG WORLD WE LIVE IN

29 DOGS SEIZED IN HUGE RSPCA RAID.

RSPCA WARN: A DOG IS FOR LIFE.

26 DOGS SEIZED

By Anya Smith

More than 26 dogs were seized from a home in Rushford, following a raid by the RSPCA and police on Thursday 9th March.

RSPCA officers, a vet and police entered the detached house in North Rushford and took the dogs and their puppies into care.

The animal charity applied for a warrant because they were concerned about the harsh way the dogs were being treated.

The dogs were put in cages and taken in vans to the Rushford Dogs' Home, where they were given a thorough medical examination.

The RSPCA is a charitable organisation that looks after sick or injured animals.

Officers from the animal rescue charity will make the decision whether to prosecute the owner of the 26 dogs and puppies.

PC Woof was part of the police team who raided the property. He commented, "the RSPCA will do a thorough investigation, look at all the evidence and decide if action is to be taken against the owner of the dogs.

- For a **newspaper report** – use a <u>**HEADLINE**</u> and a **STRAP LINE**.

- **Recount** the *main details* of the story – *where, when, why, which, who?*

- **Structure** your work. Write your   points *in the order* they happened.

- **Organise** your work into short paragraphs.

- Help the reader to visualise the scene, with **detailed description**.

- Add further **background information**.

- Use **quotes** from people who were there.

- Add a **comment** from the writer.

Now write the text for a newspaper report about a crime that has occurred. You could use the Great Train Robbery at the end of this book or maybe the headline – '20 Cats Seized'.

Have you ever played a party game called 'murder in the dark'? Some cards are prepared in advance. All the party guests take one. The guest with the card 'detective' on it leaves the room. The lights are turned off. The guest with the card 'murderer' on it taps a guest and they fall down on the floor screaming. The lights go on. Now the detective has to interrogate all the people in the room, until he finds who did it.

- Can you name some famous detectives?

- Can you name a book, a film or a television programme featuring a famous detective? Write down what the plots are of these books or films.

- Write your own detective story. Think about the crime, the clues, the witnesses and solving 'who done it'.

ROBBERY
Crime of the 20th Century

When: August 1963

Where: a village called Cheddington in Buckinghamshire

What happened? The mail train carrying vast sums of bank notes travelling from London to Glasgow was held up.

Who did this? A famous criminal masterminded the crime. His gang consisted of 15 hardened criminals and other 'helpers' who were not directly involved.

How did they do it? The gang put up a fake signal on the line. The train stopped. The criminals gagged and tied up the train driver. They drove the train down the line a mile. They unloaded a hoard of money - £2,631,684 in bank notes, which is worth more than 40 million today! They handcuffed staff and made their get away.

What did they do next? They loaded a waiting lorry and travelled to Leatherslade Farm – which had been purchased for them as a hideout, by a dodgy solicitor. There they waited, playing monopoly using real money. When they heard the police had cordoned off the roads and were closing in on them, they tried to run, but was it too late?

How did they get caught? The police were tipped off by a herdsman who worked on a field near the gang's hideout. The police entered the farm and found many post office sacks, registered mail packages and bank note wrappers. They found fingerprints on a bottle of ketchup and on a monopoly board.

What sentence did they get? A number of arrests were made and 12 men were jailed. Two of the train robbers escaped from prison. One was re-caught. However, Ronnie Biggs (the most famous robber) escaped from Wandsworth Prison, only 15 months into his sentence. A furniture van was parked alongside the prison walls and a ladder dropped over the 30 foot wall into the prison during outside exercise time. The stolen money was never recovered.

Excerpts from a play script:

<u>A Den Of Robbers</u>

Your task is to write the missing scenes for the play script.

<u>**Scene 1:**</u>   *(the cellar of a house.)*

Bruce: Our plan is to hold up the night post train. See this map – the train will be travelling from London to Glasgow and at about 10pm it will pass Cheddington. That's where we'll take it.

All: **Yes Boss!**

Bruce: Joe – you and Bob will set up a fake railway signal. It will turn red as the train approaches. The train will stop. The driver may get out. Over power him.

Joe: What… kill him…?

Bruce: Whatever you like. Gag him – tie him up – leave him in the bushes, but don't let him talk to anyone. Hand cuff the workers at the station – in case they see there is a problem and alert the police.

You'll then drive the train Joe, because you've worked on the railway. Drive it back down the line a few miles. Ronnie will be ready to start unloading the cash. It will be in bags. Dennis will be in the get away lorry. So the plan is - we load the bags into the lorry and make a quick getaway.

Dan has acquired Leatherslade Farm. You'll drive there – it's quite remote – with a tree-lined drive. We'll unload the cash at dusk. That's all there is to it. We'll be rich!

(The robbery takes place according to plan. The men lay low at their remote hide out.)

(at the farm.)

Bruce: I've just heard on the radio – the police are searching the area.

| **Dennis:** | I wouldn't worry. This farm is so remote. They'll never find us here. |

| **Ronnie:** | Dan - the solicitor has just phoned – he says the village is swarming with police. They've blocked off the main road. |

| **Bruce:** | We're going to have to make a run for it. It's only a matter of time before they search the farm. |

| **Dennis:** | Here put the monopoly board away. |

| **Bruce:** | No, there's no time to tidy up. Lets just get out quick. |

| <u>**Scene 2:**</u> | *(At the police station, two police men are going through the witness statement from the robbery. They are determined to catch the robbers.)* |

| **Detective 1:** | What did they say? |

| | *(He reads the witness statement.)* |

| **Detective 2:** | The criminal told the witness that he was going to gagg him to make sure that he didn't speak to anyone for thirty minutes. He told him if he talked he would be... |

| **Detective 1:** | Only, thirly minutes – that means the crooks must still be in a radius of no more than thirty miles. Get all the premises searched in a thirty miles radius of London. Get in touch with every police station and block off all main roads. |

| **Detective 2:** | We must act swiftly so the robbers don't get away. Search warehouses, cellars and farms… any remote places they could hide out |

| | *(later…)* |

| **Detective 1:** | Sarg, we've got quite a few fingerprints at the station. These match up with master criminal Bruce. We've got an address for him. |

| **Detective 2:** | Get round to his house now. |

Now write the scene for the arrest.

Scene 3

Fill in the missing dialogue

<u>**Scene 4:**</u>	*(Judge sits in his chair and jury sit on the benches. Court proceedings begin.)*

The Court: I hereby charge you with the offence of robbing the London to Glasgow post train on Wednesday August 16th 1963.

(Defendant to speak)

Do you have anything to say in your defence?

Joe: I was at home, watching T.V. on that day.

(Witness comes forward)

Witness: It was definitely that man who grabbed me and put the gag round my mouth. He said he'd kill me if I struggled. Then, he got into my cab and drove the train back up the line. I passed out after this and I don't remember anything else........................
....
....

Defence lawyer: Your honour, I have proof that this man was at home on..............
....
....

Prosecuting lawyer: I would argue to the contrary, your honour. This man matches the description of the man who wilfully grabbed the train driver, beat him black and blue, put handcuffs on him and left him tied up ....
....

(A long time later – after a lot of evidence and witnesses have been heard, the jury go out to consider the verdict.)

Judge: After having considered the evidence, I find you guilty. I hereby sentence you to 25 years in prison.
(Joe is led away in handcuffs.)

Joe: ....
....

Prison Officer: ....

Write the final scene: Ronnie plans his escape from prison.

- *When does he escape?*
- *How does he scale the wall?*
- *How does he get away?*
- *Where does he go?*
- *Is he ever found?*

Write an article to help children understand how the law system works. Use the information below:

What do you have to do to become a lawyer?
- A person who studies law is called a lawyer.
- He/She studies law at university and gets a degree.
- When he or she qualifies, he or she can be a family lawyer, a criminal lawyer or a civil lawyer.

What do laws do?
- Every society has laws to keep people safe.
- Criminal lawyers protect people from criminals, such as burglars who steal possessions.
- Civic lawyers help people settle disputes and decide who is right. For example, if you bought a car and it broke down the next day.

Why do people serve prison sentences?
- It is a punishment for people who commit serious crimes.
- It protects people from danger.
- Prison helps criminals reform their ways and stops them getting into trouble again.

How were criminals treated in the past?
- Some were executed and some transported to other countries by boat. Some countries still execute people today - as a punishment for crimes like murder.

What else do lawyers do?
- Lawyers decide who is to blame in an accident.
- In international crime, lawyers return people to their own countries to face punishment.

What happens in a courtroom?
- If a criminal is accused of a serious crime, he or she has the right to a trial with a jury.
- From the electoral roll, twelve men and women are chosen to sit on the jury.
- A lawyer represents the person prosecuting the criminal. He tries to convince the jury that the defendant (person accused) is guilty. Another lawyer (representing the defence) tries to convince the jury that the person is innocent.
- Witnesses tell the court what they saw at the time of the crime.
- The jury listens to the evidence and decides whether he or she is innocent or guilty.
- The judge helps the jury understand the laws relating to a crime.
- If the criminal is guilty, the judge decides on the punishment.

Write your article here.

Write an introduction: why we have laws?

Point 1: punishment for criminals

Point 2: punishment in the past.

Point 3: punishment in a trial by jury

Conclusion: I have found out that...

Made in the USA
Monee, IL
07 July 2026

56644836R00015